Quick-and-Easy
Crazy Quilt Patchwork

With 14 Projects

Dixie Haywood

D0131511

DOVER PUBLICATIONS, INC.

New York

For
Brent, who made it necessary
and
Dana, Todd, and Bob, who made it possible

Acknowledgments

Even a personal book such as this is not possible without the aid of many people. I am especially grateful to Michael Stipek, who transformed my demonstrations in thread and fabric into clear illustrations; to my husband, Bob, for hours of photographing and KP; and to Will Andrepont, for his film-printing abilities. In addition, thanks belong to Donna and Doyle Orrell, Melinda and Michael Keenan, Pat and Larry Smith, Avens Furniture, and the Butterick Fashion Marketing Company.

Long before this book was conceived, the encouragement of Moreen Goldman, Jean Kehl, and Zona Wickham led to the development of my ideas. And it was the enthusiasm and questions of students and customers that led me from the sewing machine to the typewriter.

Copyright © 1977 by Dixie Haywood.
All rights reserved under Pan American and International Copyright Conventions.

Published in Canada by General Publishing Company, Ltd., 30 Lesmill Road, Don Mills, Toronto, Ontario.
Published in the United Kingdom by Constable and Company, Ltd., 3 The Lanchesters, 162–164 Fulham Palace Road, London W6 9ER.

Quick-and-Easy Crazy Quilt Patchwork: With 14 Projects is a slightly abridged republication of *The Contemporary Crazy Quilt Project Book*, first published by Crown Publishers, Inc., New York, in 1977. The text has been reset for this edition, the layout has been redone and the four color pages in the original edition have been omitted.

Manufactured in the United States of America
Dover Publications, Inc., 31 East 2nd Street, Mineola, N.Y. 11501

Library of Congress Cataloging-in-Publication Data

Haywood, Dixie.
    [Contemporary crazy quilt project book]
    Quick-and-easy crazy quilt patchwork : with 14 projects / Dixie Haywood.
        p.   cm. — (Dover needlework series)
    "Slightly abridged republication of The contemporary crazy quilt project book, first published by Crown Publishers, Inc., New York, in 1977"—T.p. verso.
    Includes index.
    ISBN 0-486-27106-4 (pbk.)
    1. Patchwork. 2. Crazy quilts. I. Title. II. Series.
TT835.H35   1992
746.46—dc20   91-42783
                                                            CIP

Contents

1.

A Short Look at the Victorian Crazy Quilt

In the second half of the nineteenth century, the Victorian crazy quilt came into fashion with a vengeance. Earlier bed quilts had undoubtedly been made of odd-shaped pieces stitched together, but they were a far cry from the Victorian crazy quilt, made of velvets, satins, ribbons, fine wools, and other fabrics considered elegant. The fabric was applied to a backing with embroidery that was frequently spectacular; many times the fabric seems to disappear under the onslaught of stitchery.

A typical Victorian crazy quilt, dated "86–93." The embroidery is lavish, covering both the edges and the center of much of the fabric. 60" × 60". Collection of the author.

Their use peaking in the period from 1870 to 1900, Victorian crazy quilts came into fashion at a time when factory bedding was beginning to be generally available, at least in settled areas where people had cash for such purchases. Crazy quilting, a leisure activity, was quite different from the practical necessity of providing warm bedding that motivated traditional quilt makers. I think it fair to assume, however, that the two activities went on simultaneously in many households.

I was tempted to call this chapter "A Kind Word for the Crazy Quilt," since there are so few kind words for the Victorian crazy quilt among writers on the American quilt. At best, American Victorian crazy quilts are damned with faint praise: words frequently used are a "brontosaurus of American patchwork," "evolutionary dead end," or "in bad taste," "incoherent," and "decadent."

I agree with many appraisals of the Victorian crazy quilt, especially when they are judged as quilts per se. As quilts they are useless—the fabric is often fragile and is usually unwashable, batting is rarely inserted, and they are neither warm nor functional. But they were not made to be used as bed quilts, and it seems unfair to judge the Victorian crazy quilt by the same criteria as a patchwork or appliqué quilt.

I believe Victorian crazy quilts can best be appreci-ated as fabric collages that served as showcases for the maker's skill in fancy needlework. They should be judged on that basis. To paraphrase an old nursery rhyme, when they were done well, they were magnificent; when they were bad, they were horrid!

I have seen crazy quilts that were made on the western frontier when it was still rough pioneer country, and my imagination is drawn to the women who made them. Unlike those of their city sisters farther east, their long days were filled with hard and sometimes dangerous work. It surely must have been difficult to justify time for such impractical activity, even to preserve family memories in fabric. I somehow think the justification was not only the status of having a crazy quilt draped over a piece of parlor furniture, displaying the maker's ability with a needle, but also the hunger for something colorful and, yes, even impractical.

It seems to me that the charm of the Victorian crazy quilt is more emotional than critical. True, there are many crazy quilts in which the fabric and stitchery transcend fussiness and gentility to become folk art at its best. But what is also fascinating is the hundreds of hours of work for its own sake. How extravagant! In our too-busy lives, it leaves us in awe and explains much of the enchantment this "brontosaurus of American patchwork" has for us.

A Victorian crazy quilt showing more planning than most. Textile painted scenes are on several pieces of fabric. 67½″ × 77½″. Collection of the author.

II.

Contemporary Crazy Quilting

I continue to be charmed by the old crazy quilts, with their rich textures and colors and beautiful stitchery. When I started designing, however, I was seeking function as well as charm. The result is what I have come to call contemporary crazy quilting.

Contemporary crazy quilting, unlike the traditional style, is actually quilting; that is, it is a "cloth sandwich" with a middle layer of batting. The batting gives the rich texture that in the Victorian crazy quilt was furnished by lovely, but often delicate, fabrics. It also gives padding that makes it possible to use the technique for objects such as glasses cases, tea cozies, pot holders, placemats, and tablecloths. And batting provides warmth, making possible quilts that are practical as well as beautiful.

Compared to the hand methods of earlier times, contemporary crazy quilting is quickly done. This technique appeals to quilt lovers who lack the skill or patience for the precision demanded by traditional patchwork and appliqué, since the basic process requires neither. It works especially well for shapes that are difficult to lay out in the strict geometry of traditional patchwork patterns. Best of all, contemporary crazy quilting allows unlimited potential for original interpretation.

The basis for making any item by this method involves putting together a "blank" in the appropriate shape. The blank consists of blank fabric and batting cut to the same size and stitched together. Crazy quilting is then machine stitched onto the blank. The crazy quilting can be done by hand if no machine is available, but there is no advantage to working by hand in this process; if anything, machine stitching enhances the quilt aspect. No machine stitching shows in the finished piece.

The choice of a suitable backing fabric for the blank depends on the object being made. Where body is needed, as in a purse or glasses case, regular Pellon* is

*Pellon is the name of a brand of nonwoven interfacing. Any similar interfacing may be used.

used. The weight of the Pellon depends on how much firmness is desired, but it is important not to use the all-bias variety, since it does not hold a firm shape. In clothing, where minimum bulk is desirable, a lightweight cotton lining fabric works well. For most other projects, a muslin-weight cotton is a good choice, and this is a way to use up those odd pieces of fabric.

It is crucial that the backing fabric be preshrunk. If you are using unbleached muslin, I recommend washing it twice, because sometimes it continues to shrink on the second washing. When I have it, I like to use salvageable portions of worn sheets. The weight is right, their washability is unquestionable, and I can feel virtuous about recycling.

I use only polyester batting, and find the bonded type easiest to cut and handle. Batting is available in different weights and degrees of puffiness. It is important to pick a weight appropriate for the purpose. I use a light type in clothing. For placemats and tablecloths I use a medium-weight batting that will not be so puffy that dishes might be unstable on it. For most things, however, I like to use the heaviest batting available. Lightweight batting can be used in multiple layers, so you can experiment with effects that different weights of batting give. It's a good idea to decrease the batting weight as the weight of the fabric used increases, unless you are aiming for a bulky effect.

When you have constructed the blank, pick out the fabric you want to use. Since most of the patterns I have worked out have been for useful objects, I have been interested in using fabrics for crazy quilting that are easily cared for and relatively durable. I use with success fabrics ranging from eyelet to corduroy. My students have done some imaginative things using double knits, upholstery fabrics, and worn denims.

Be sure your fabric is preshrunk and colorfast. Press it before you start sewing. Don't iron fabric once it is quilted to the batting, unless you want to flatten it. I usually cut or tear large pieces of fabric into six- to eight-inch widths for easier handling. Scraps are left as they are. Although most shapes are cut after the fabric has been sewn in place, the shape and size of scraps often suggest placement. In fact, my best results have come as the scraps pile up in odd shapes; a large, uncut piece of fabric seems to inhibit my imagination!

Although there is no limit to the amount of different fabrics you can use in a single piece of crazy quilting, I like to pick out two or three prints and two solid fabrics that go well together. If not enough fabrics are used, there is the possibility of getting into a situation where you have to cross a section of crazy quilting with one of the same fabrics in the section. Too many fabrics can give your finished piece an incoherent look.

Small prints are more effective than large ones, because cutting a large print often makes the print out of proportion to the size of the piece, and the fabric pattern thus becomes meaningless and confusing to the overall design. Stitchery shows up best on solid fabrics, so it is important to balance the pieces of print fabric with solid colors that will showcase your stitchery. Even with the added texture of the batting, crazy quilting still derives much of its charm from the stitchery on it; stitchery brings the whole piece to life.

Developing a feel for the shapes used in crazy quilting can be achieved only by practice, but my students are always surprised at how quickly they start seeing design possibilities as they play with piecing the blank. One suggestion is to think small, for most beginners start by using too many large pieces. Another suggestion is to think in terms of curves. They are not only interesting from a design standpoint, but are also a solution to the box you can get into when too many angles come together. Curves cannot be machine-stitched into place. They are pinned on and closed with stitchery later, so it works best to have at least one fabric along the curve be a solid color. Long, narrow strips are often effective, but I use almost no squares or rectangles. (An exception to this is the tea cozy, but it is a variation of the technique using planned shapes and is not strictly crazy quilting.)

The excitement of crazy quilting comes when your own design takes shape. Don't worry that you may have no talent for shape, color, or texture; it's at least 90 percent practice. The first piece is the hardest. Get out those scraps of fabric and start!

Cut batting and blank fabric to the desired shape. Choose the fabric to be used, and press it.

Machine baste the batting and blank fabric together to form the blank. For the easiest stitching, sew with the blank fabric on top, using the seam allowance desired for the finished piece.

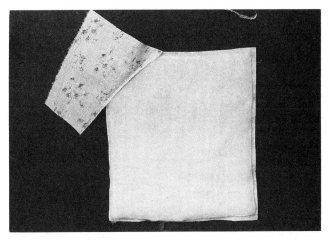

Place the next fabric to be used, uncut, right side down over the first piece and machine sew, using a long stitch. Do not pin the top piece.

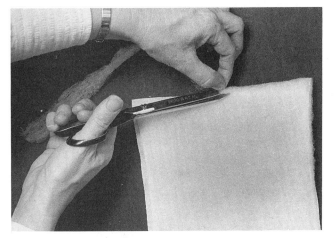

When bulk in the seams is undesirable, trim the batting from the seam allowance. (Read the directions for the project before trimming—sometimes batting is needed in the seam allowance.)

Open the fabric to the right side and cut it to the desired shape if necessary. Pin open the piece to keep it from moving out of place as the next piece is sewn over it.

Turn the batting side up. Cut the first piece of fabric to the desired shape and pin it, right side up, in the upper left-hand corner. Do not place the pin where you will machine-stitch across it, as it may cause a pleat to be formed. Left-handed sewers may prefer to work from the upper right-hand corner.

Continue, sewing with the right sides together, opening and cutting to shape, then pinning in place. Generally work from the upper left corner to the lower right.

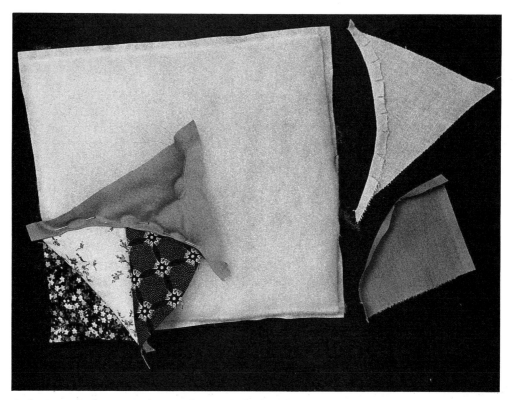

Only straight lines can be machine-stitched. When you wish to add a curve, pin it in place right side up. The seam will be closed with stitchery when the piece is finished. To achieve a smooth curve, clip the concave curves, and trim and press the convex curves.

When sewing a light-colored fabric over a darker one, set the light fabric to cover the edge of the darker one completely, taking a deeper seam than usual if necessary. When the light fabric is opened, you don't want the seam allowance of the dark fabric to show through underneath. This photo illustrates the *incorrect* placement of a light fabric.

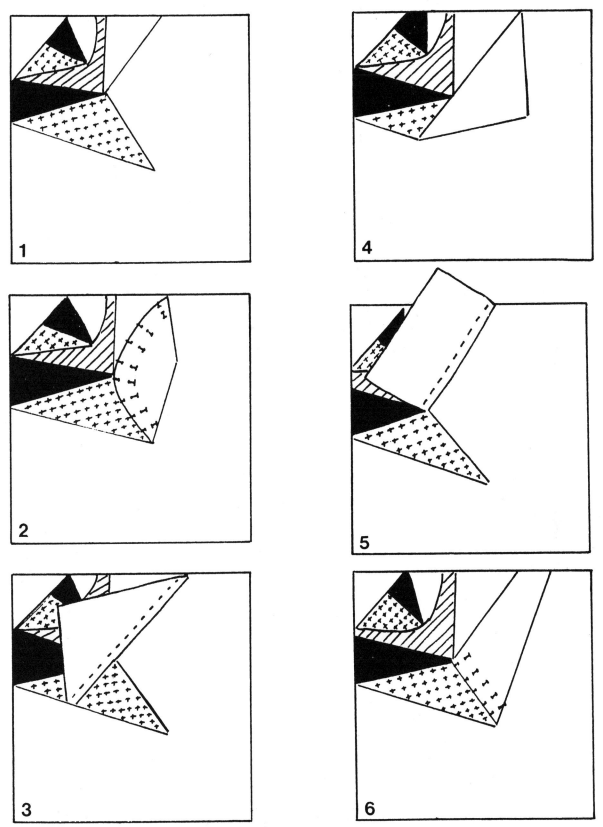

A piecing problem that most beginners encounter is how to handle a right angle (1). Three possible solutions: Pin a curve over the angle and close it with stitchery (2); sew across the angle to form a straight seam, then trim out the excess fabric (3 and 4); sew the piece to one side of the angle, turn under the second side and pin it, then close it with stitchery (5 & 6).

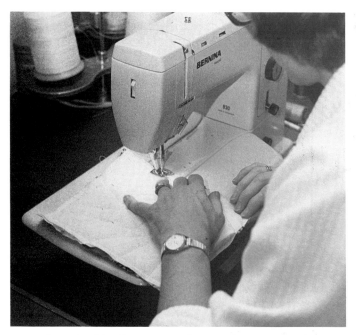

When the blank is covered, trim the crazy quilting to the same size as the blank and machine baste around the piece on the wrong side, using a slightly narrower seam allowance than will be used in the finished item. Or, if you have a machine with a zigzag stitch, it works even better to zigzag-stitch along the edge.

You are now ready to apply stitchery and construct your project.

*A **close-up** of a section of a Victorian crazy quilt, showing the profusion and variety of stitches.*

III.

Stitchery for Crazy Quilting

Stitchery is the finishing touch that brings your crazy quilting to life. There are really no rules as to what stitches to use and where to put them, though as I indicated in Chapter 2, stitchery is more effective on solid colors than on prints. The fabric in Victorian crazy quilts was put together with stitchery, so every edge was covered. I have found that unnecessary and even undesirable with contemporary crazy quilting. Stitchery is an accent that enhances colors in the fabric and texture of the batting, but it should not dominate.

Experiment with different threads. I use cotton embroidery thread most often, embroidering with all six strands. I have also used a nylon velvet thread that is available at some needlepoint shops, acrylic yarn in different weights, and rayon embroidery thread.

The following stitches are the ones I use most frequently. Try them out, add some of your favorites, and keep an eye out for new stitches to add to your repertoire.

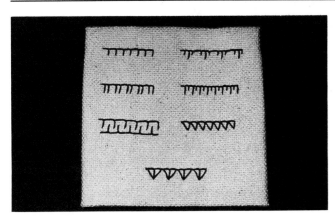

The basic blanket stitch and variations.

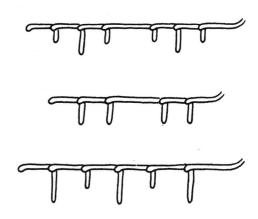

Variations of the blanket stitch are useful and add variety. Vary the length and spacing of stitches.

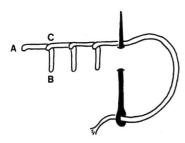

The blanket stitch. Bring the needle through at the line to be followed (A). Insert the needle at a right angle to the thread at the desired depth (B) and cross over the thread (C). Pull to form a loop.

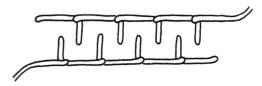

Work one row of the blanket stitch. Turn the piece upside down and work back. This is effective in two colors.

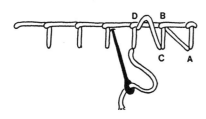

Work the blanket stitch. Then work back with diagonal stitches.

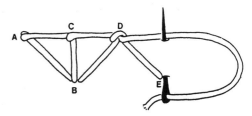

For another buttonhole variation, bring the needle through at the line to be followed (A). Insert the needle from B to A, B to C, B to D. The next group starts from E to D and follows the same pattern.

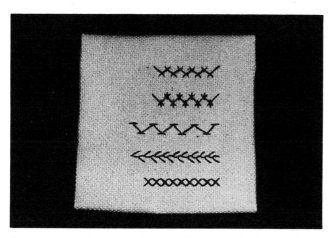

From top to bottom: *Herringbone stitch, herringbone star stitch, chevron stitch, feather stitch, cross-stitch.*

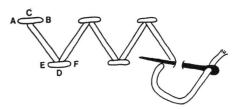

Chevron stitch. Bring the needle through at A and insert it at B, taking a backstitch to C. Insert it at D, with a backstitch to E, then insert it at F and bring the thread out again at D.

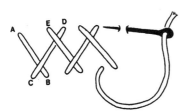

Herringbone stitch. Bring the needle through at A and insert it at B, taking a short backstitch to C. Repeat the backstitch from D to E. Continue in this manner, working left to right.

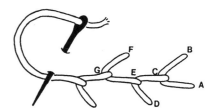

Feather stitch. This stitch seems to be the one that people have the most trouble learning. It seems easiest to understand if thought of as an alternating blanket stitch worked diagonally. Bring the needle through at A and insert it at B, exiting across the thread at C. Pull to form a loop. Insert the needle at D, exiting across the thread at E. Continue from F to G.

Herringbone star stitch. This is one I arrived at by doodling with thread, and it is one of my favorites. Work the basic herringbone stitch, then work back across the backstitches as shown.

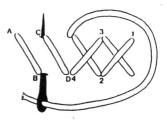

Cross-stitch. This is a difficult stitch to do evenly without threads to count, but it is effective on some fabrics. Working evenly, making a row of parallel stitches, A to B, C to D, etc. Then work back, 1 to 2, 3 to 4, forming crosses.

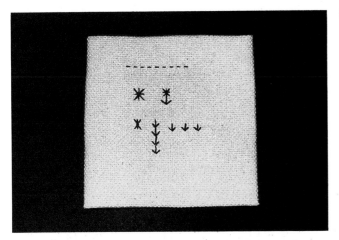

From top to bottom, left to right: *Running stitch, star stitch, star flower, sheaf stitch, fern stitch, fern stitch variation.*

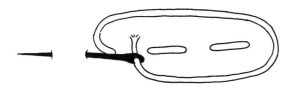

Running stitch. Here's a simple one that is useful to outline pieces too small to work a pattern stitch on.

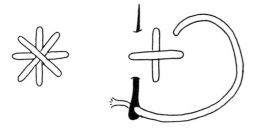

Star stitch. This is an accent stitch that I use for a personal signature. It is simply four straight stitches crossed.

Star flower. This is another nice accent stitch, combining a star stitch with a fern stitch.

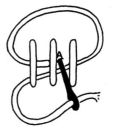

Sheaf stitch. This is usually worked with the vertical stitches close together. I like them expanded somewhat for use on crazy quilting. Make three parallel straight stitches, evenly spaced. Bring the needle out at **A**, loop around all straight stitches twice, and insert it at **A**. Do not catch the fabric when looping the stitches.

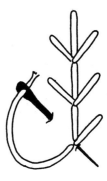

Fern stitch. Although this resembles the feather stitch, it is simpler. Work three straight stitches from the same starting point.

Fern stitch variation. This is effective when worked along an edge, either as shown or upside down.

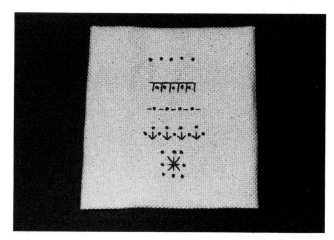

The French knot and examples of it combined with other stitches.

French knot. Bring the needle through where the knot is desired. Wrap the thread around the needle two or three times, depending on the thread used. Hold the thread firmly and insert the needle near the place from which it emerged.

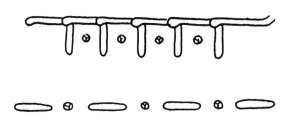

The French knot is nice when combined with other stitches. Here it is shown with the blanket stitch and the running stitch.

The French knot with a fern stitch. This illustration shows the fern stitches spaced farther apart than in the first photo of them. The photograph shows another variation with the fern stitches closer.

The French knot with the star stitch.

IV.

The Project Section

The projects in this section range from simple to complex. I hope in this way to give novices projects on which to build their skill and confidence, as well as to give more experienced quilters challenges commensurate with their ability. Use the general instructions in Chapter 2 as a guide and follow the specific directions for the project you wish to make.

The seam allowance for these patterns is ¼″, except in the case of clothing. On most sewing machines this is the distance from the needle to the edge of the presser foot. By using the presser foot as a guide, you can work accurately and avoid the necessity for a lot of trimming.

The yardage needed depends on the number of fabrics used and the amount of cutting done. You can generally figure that an amount of fabric equal to 1¼ to 1⅓ the area of the blank will be adequate. On the larger projects I have indicated the yardage used in making the items.

When you are trying to space out a limited amount of one or two fabrics, mentally divide the blank into sections and allot the fabric proportionately. This way, the limited fabric will be spaced throughout the blank and you can fill in with other fabrics that are in better supply.

Project

1

Pincushion

Cutting Directions:

Blank fabric and backing for the pincushion: 4½″ square.

Supplies Needed:

Washed sand, available at builders supply and aquarium outlets

Notes:

Both the blank and the backing should be a firm fabric.

The pincushion is an exception to the general instructions in that it does not use batting on the blank, because batting corrodes pins and needles left in it. The pincushion is filled with sand, which has two advantages: it keeps pins and needles sharp, and it gives weight to the pincushion so it isn't easily knocked to the floor. It also makes a good paperweight.

Crazy quilt the blank according to the general instructions, but without batting. Embroider as desired.

With the right sides together, sew the back to the blank on three sides, extending it around corners about ½" on the fourth side. This makes it easier to fill without spilling sand.

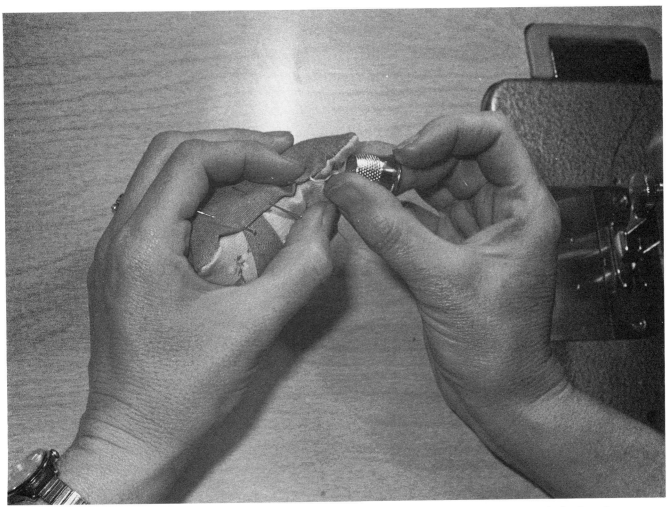

Turn the pincushion, then fill it with sand to the desired fullness. Close the opening securely by hand.

Project

2

Place Setting

Cutting Directions:

For each placemat: blank fabric, batting, and lining
For each coaster: blank fabric, batting, and lining
For each napkin tie: lightweight all-bias Pellon
For each napkin: napkin fabric and 1⅔ yards of two-inch bias, cut of napkin fabric

Notes:

1. Trim the batting from the seam allowance on the placemat and coaster.
2. Use a light- or medium-weight batting.
3. No batting is used in the napkin tie. This is the only design in the book in which bias Pellon is used, and care must be used not to pull it out of shape as you work.

This place setting is a fine beginner's project. It looks like quite an undertaking, but it couldn't be simpler.

Pattern diagrams for the place setting. (One square equals one inch.)

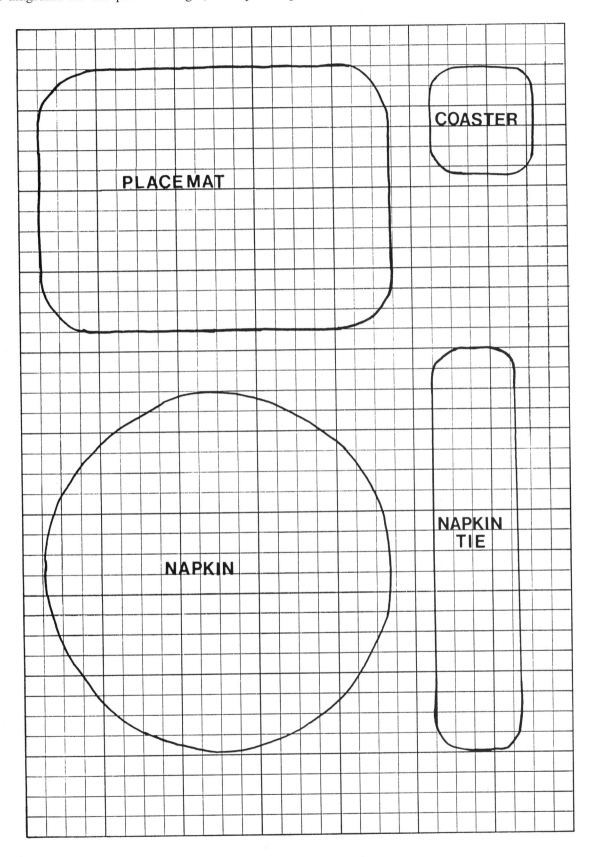

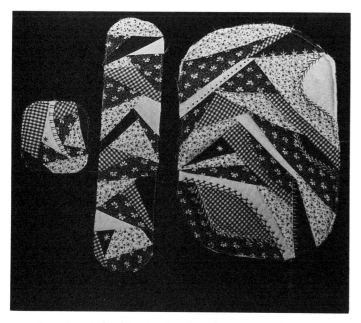

Construct the blanks for the placemat and coaster according to the general directions. Crazy quilt the placemat, coaster, and Pellon for the napkin tie. Embroider as desired.

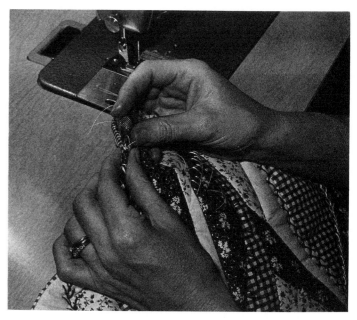

Turn all pieces right side out and close the openings by hand. Press the edges *lightly* on the wrong side.

With the right sides together, stitch the lining to the placemat and coaster, leaving an opening for turning. Fold the napkin tie lengthwise and stitch it, leaving an opening.

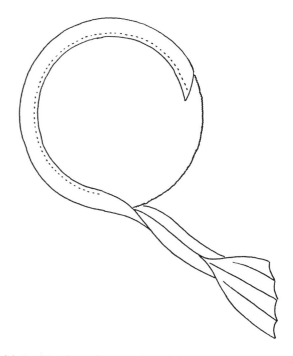

Fold the bias lengthwise, then fold both raw edges into the center. Apply the bias to the edge of the napkin, taking care not to stretch it out of shape.

Project

3

Glasses Case

Cutting Directions:

Pellon, regular weight, nonbias type: 8″ × 8½″
Batting: 8″ × 8½″
Lining fabric: 7½″ × 8″

Notes:

1. Do not trim batting from the seam allowance when constructing the blank.

2. Keep in mind when crazy quilting that the glasses case will be folded down the middle. You are constructing a two-sided object rather than a flat one, and the design should be balanced.

3. Spray with Scotchgard when finished and respray after each washing.

Pellon is used on the glasses case for the blank fabric. The combination of Pellon and batting gives good protection to glasses.

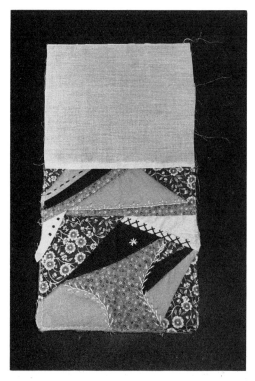

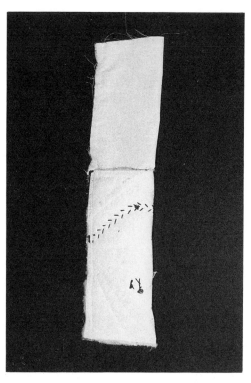

Construct the blank according to the general instructions, then crazy quilt it and embroider as desired. Sew the lining to the top of the completed blank.

Fold the blank lengthwise, right sides together, and stitch down the side of the lining and case, and across the bottom of the case.

Turn right side out, fold under the raw edges of the lining bottom, and stitch it closed. Push the lining to the inside of the glasses case. The crazy quilting should extend inside for a short distance.

4

Pot Holder

Cutting Directions:

Blank fabric: 1, 9″ square
Batting: 2, 9″ square
Backing: 1, 10½″ square

Supplies Needed:

Bone or wooden ring

Notes:

1. Do not trim batting from the seam allowance when constructing the blank.
2. If two layers of batting are difficult to handle in your sewing machine, construct the blank with one layer and crazy quilt it. Machine baste or zigzag the second batting to the back of the blank before embroidering, and embroider through all layers to hold the second batting in place.
3. These directions give a back with mitered corners that rolls around the front. If you prefer to use a bias binding, which can be applied faster but which rounds off the corners, cut the back the same size as the blank.
4. The back should be of a print or dark fabric so that the embroidery on the wrong side of the blank will not show through.

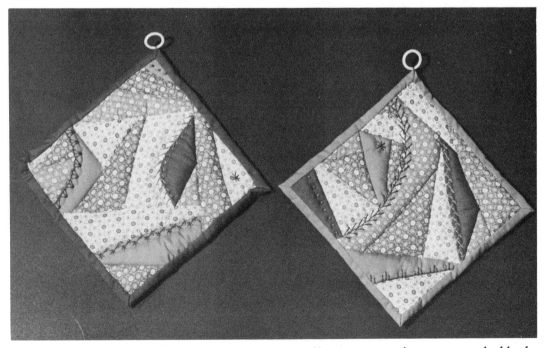

This makes a large, practical pot holder. Two layers of batting are used to construct the blank. Polyester batting conducts heat to some extent, so it takes double layering to make certain that the pot holder is practical as well as decorative.

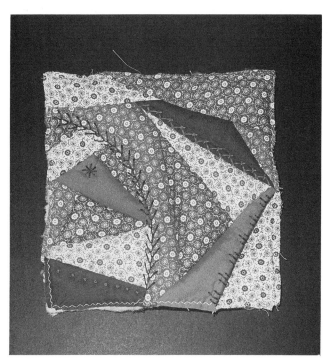

Construct the blank using two layers of batting, then crazy quilt it and embroider as desired.

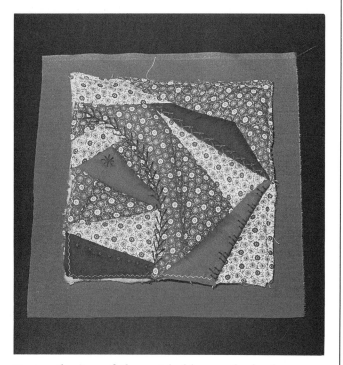

Center the top of the pot holder on the back, wrong sides together, and pin it securely.

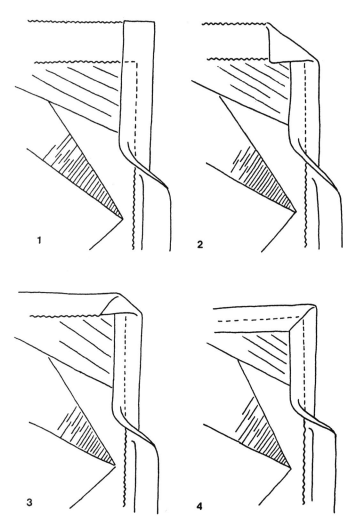

To miter the edges: (1) Turn under ⅜″ of seam allowance on the back, rolling ⅜″ around the front. (2) Fold the back to a right angle at the corner. (3) Turn under ⅜″ of seam allowance on the next side. (4) Fold over the front, forming a miter at the corner.

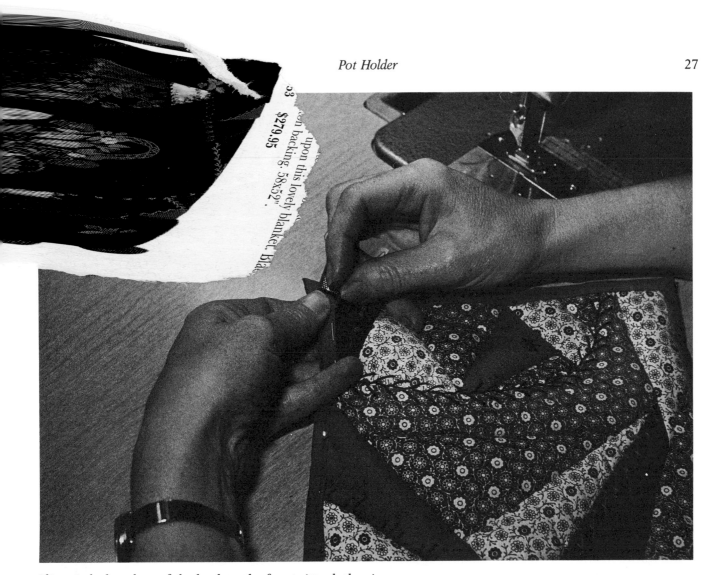

Slip stitch the edges of the back to the front. Attach the ring.

Project

5

Reversible
Toaster Cover

Cutting Directions:

Sides: Cut 2 each of blank fabric, batting, and lining,
   from pattern.
Center: Cut 1 each of fabric choice, batting, and lining,
   6½″ × 24½″.
Ruffle: Cut 2 widths of fabric, 4″ wide.
Handle: Cut 1″ × 6½″ of center fabric and lining fabric.

Notes:

Do not trim batting from the seam allowance when
constructing the blank.

When you want a change in your kitchen, turn the toaster cover inside out!

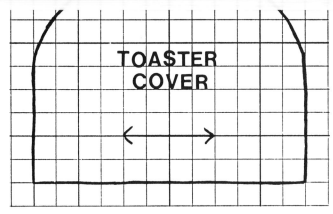

The pattern diagram for the sides of the toaster cover. (One square equals one inch.)

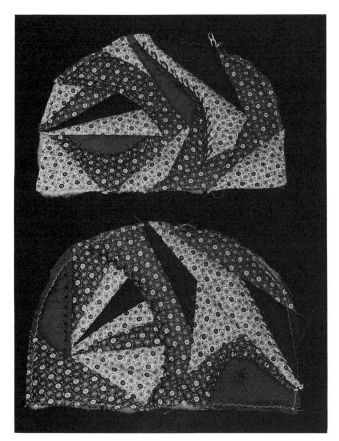

Construct blanks for the sides of the toaster cover according to the general directions and then crazy quilt, embroidering as desired.

Machine baste the batting to the wrong side of the center fabric, using a scant ¼″ seam allowance. The seam line should cover the basting when constructed. Fold the handle lengthwise and then stitch it. Turn, press, and attach it across the middle of the center section.

With the right sides together, sew the sides to each side of the center section. Pin the edges even at the bottom, then match the middle of the center section to the top of the sides and ease around the curve. Stitch, following the basting lines on the center section.

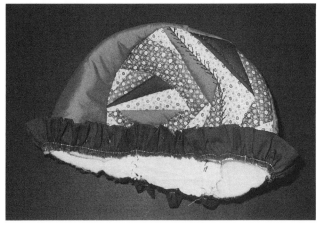

Sew the ruffle fabric into a loop. Press it in half lengthwise, with the wrong sides together. Gather to fit the bottom, and attach it.

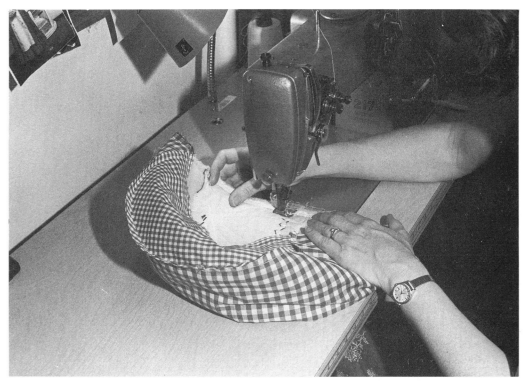

Construct the lining in the same manner as the top. Pull the lining over the toaster cover, right sides together, and stitch around the bottom, following the ruffle's stitching line and leaving one end open across the center section.

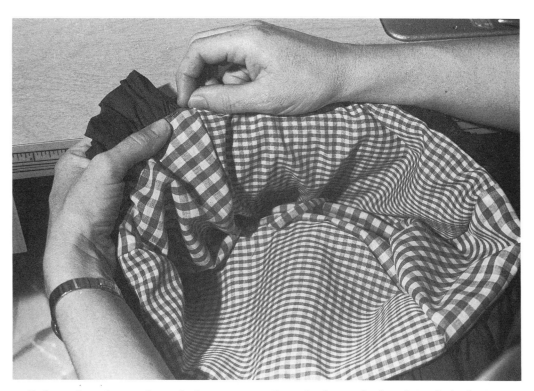

Pull the right side out through the opening. Close the lining by hand. Tack the lining to both sides of the center, sewing under the handle so that the stitches won't show.

Project

6

Tea Cozy

Cutting Directions:

Cut 2 each of blank fabric, batting, and lining, from pattern.
Cut 3″ square for handle.

Supplies Needed:

1 yard of eyelet ruffle

Notes:

1. Do not trim batting from the seam allowance when constructing the blank.
2. Use a heavy batting or two layers of light batting.
3. If you prefer a double fabric ruffle, follow the directions given for the toaster cover (Project 5). Cording is also attractive around the bottom.
4. When using eyelet fabric, back it with solid-color fabric and treat it as a single piece.

Here's a variation of the technique, using planned shapes for a different effect. Eyelet is used as one of the fabrics. This is equally effective in crazy quilt piecing.

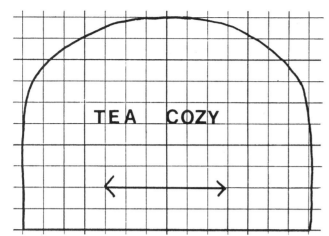

The pattern diagram for the tea cozy. (One square equals one inch.)

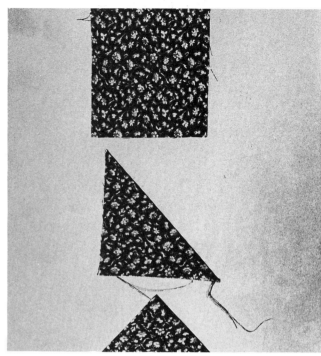

Press a 3″ square diagonally twice, to form a triangle for the handle. All raw edges will be at the bottom. Pin to the center of the top of one side of the completed blank.

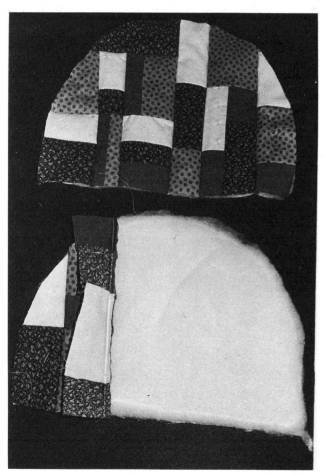

Construct the blank. Sew the fabric in squares and rectangles in vertical rows. The first row can be applied with each piece sewn through the batting. Subsequent rows are pieced and then applied to the previous row as one completed strip.

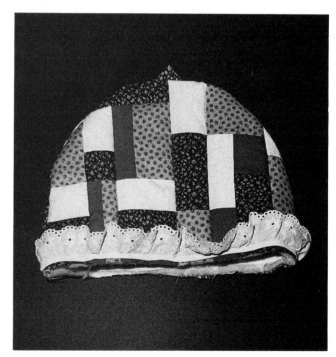

Place two sides of the tea cozy with their right sides together and then stitch. Turn it right side out and apply the ruffle to the bottom.

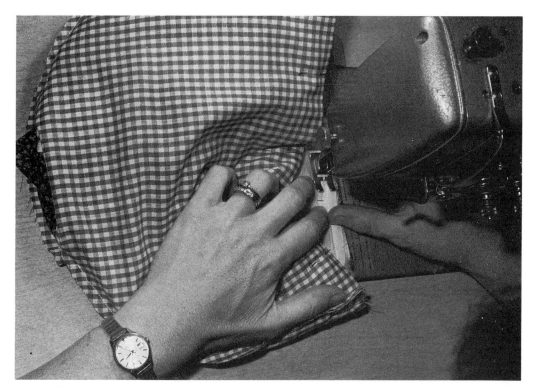

Construct the lining, leaving an opening at the top. Pull the lining over the tea cozy, right sides together, and stitch around the bottom, following the ruffle's stitching line.

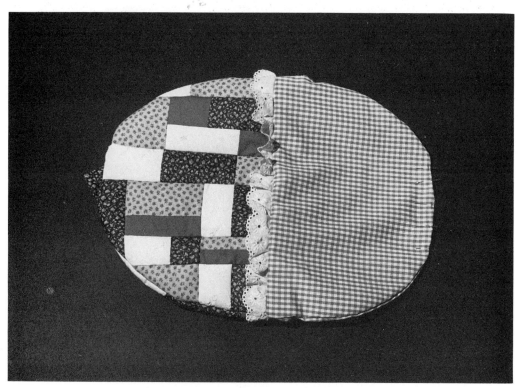

Pull the right side out through the opening in the lining. Close the lining and tack it to the inside at the top and at the side seams near the bottom.

7

Christmas Stocking

Cutting Directions:

For stocking: Cut blank fabric, batting, back, and 2 lining pieces from pattern.
For loop: Cut 1″ × 4″ piece from back fabric.

Supplies Needed:

2 yarn tassels or bells

Notes:

1. Do not trim batting from the seam allowance when constructing the blank.
2. The back of the stocking should be of a heavy fabric such as duck.

This is the first design I developed in crazy quilting, and it remains one of my favorites. It's a stocking that will last through the years.

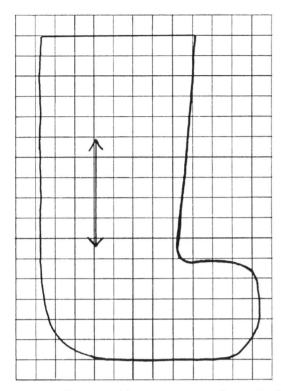

The pattern diagram. (One square equals one inch.)

Pin tassels to the toe and the front of the top.

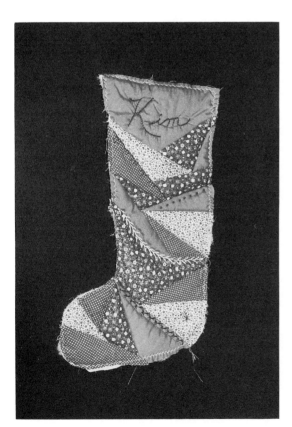

Construct the blank, then crazy quilt according to the general instructions, embroidering as desired.

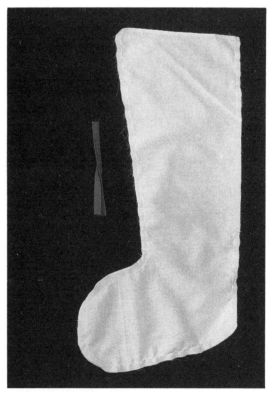

Sew the lining pieces together, leaving about a 5″ opening along the back. Clip the curves. Fold the loop fabric lengthwise, turn the raw edges to the center, and stitch it closed.

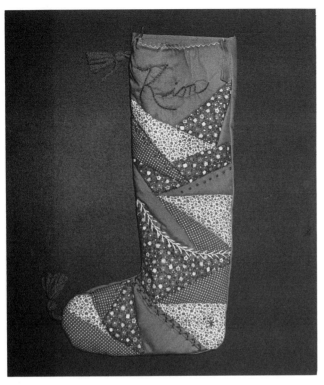

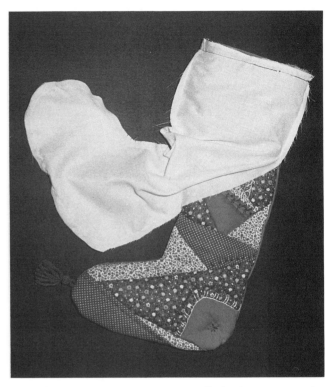

With the right sides together, stitch the back to the front, leaving the top open. Clip the curves. Turn. Pin the loop to the top of the stocking at the back seam.

With the right sides together, pull the lining over the stocking through the opening in back of the lining. Stitch together around the top, double stitching across the loop.

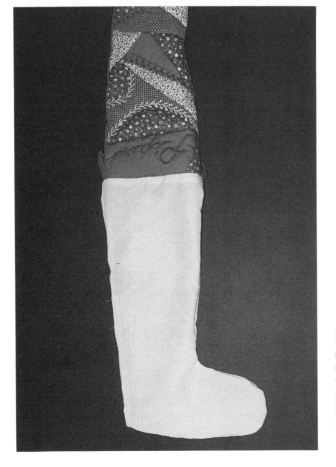

Pull the lining above the stocking, turning it right side out. Stitch the opening together. Push the lining to the inside, pressing it lightly around the top of the stocking.

8

Christmas Ornaments

Cutting Directions:

Cut a blank fabric and back for each ornament desired.

Supplies Needed:

Yarn or ribbon for loops
Small tassels or bells for diamond and bell

Here's a way to use those little scraps you have left from the Christmas stockings and the batting trimmings from the other projects. Although batting would work fine on the blanks, I don't use it, because I stuff the ornaments with batting trimmings.

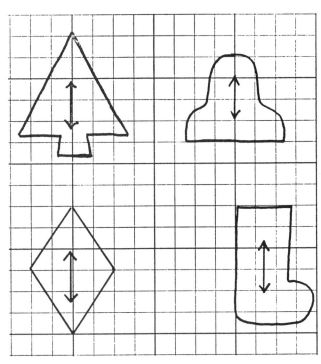

Pattern diagrams. (One square equals one inch.)

Pin yarn or ribbon to the top of the ornament on the right side. Pin the tassels on the bell and the diamond.

Crazy quilt the blanks according to the general instructions, and embroider as desired.

With the right sides together, sew the back to the front, leaving an opening. Clip the curves and angles, Turn it, stuff it with batting scraps, and close the seam.

9

Christmas Wreath

Cutting Directions:

Cut blank fabric, batting, and back from pattern.
Loop for hanging: 1½″ × 6″ of back fabric
Bow: Cut four 6″ widths of fabric.

Supplies Needed:

Approximately 1½ pounds of polyester fiberfill

Notes:

1. Do not trim batting from the seam allowance when constructing the blank.
2. The back of the wreath should be a heavy fabric such as duck. If you want to use a lighter-weight fabric, reinforce it with Pellon.

Here's the place to work in some velvets and other elegant fabrics if you wish, since you are not likely to be washing or dry cleaning this!

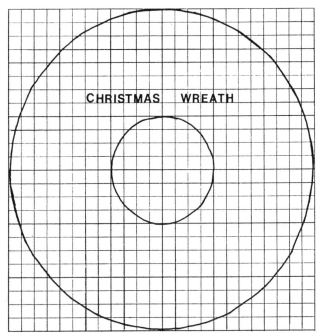

The pattern diagram. (One square equals one inch.)

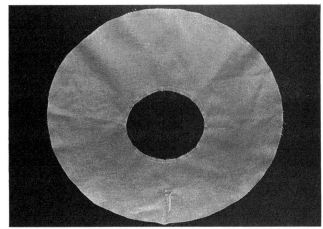

Construct a loop according to the directions for the Christmas stocking. Attach the loop securely to the back at the center of the top. Machine baste for ¼" around the inner circle of the top and back, and clip to the stitching.

With the right sides together, stitch back to front around the outside of the circle. Turn it and stuff with fiberfill. Pin the inner circle closed and close the seam securely by hand.

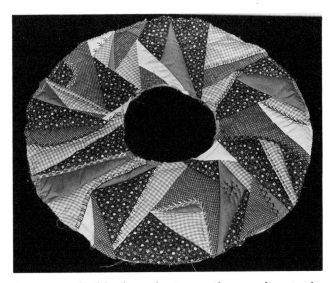

Construct the blank, and crazy quilt according to the general instructions. Embroider as desired.

Join the bow pieces into two strips. Cut the ends to a point. With the right sides together, stitch all around, leaving an opening. Turn, close the seam, and press. Tie a bow and attach it to the wreath.

10

Shopping Bag

Cutting Directions:

Body of bag: 16½" × 40". Cut one of batting, lining fabric, and heavy, nonbias Pellon.

Sides of bag: 6½" × 18½", with bottom edges rounded. Cut two each of batting, side fabric, lining fabric, and heavy, nonbias Pellon.

Handles: 2" × 15". Cut two of batting and heavy, nonbias Pellon. Cut four of the handle fabric.

Lining pocket: 8½" × 11". Cut two of the lining and one of Pellon.

Pocket reinforcement: 2" × 16½". Cut two of Pellon.

Notes:

1. Do not trim batting from the seam allowance when constructing the blank.
2. Spray with Scotchgard when finished and after each washing.

Save a tree; carry a shopping bag instead of using wrapping paper! With a plastic lining, this would make a good beach or diaper bag.

Construct the blank with Pellon and batting, and crazy quilt it according to the general instructions. Embroider as desired.

Construct the sides. Sandwich the batting between Pellon and the side fabric, and machine baste it together. Construct the handles. Layer the Pellon (*bottom*), the batting, and two pieces of handle fabric laid right sides together, and stitch, sewing in the same direction on both sides to avoid twisting. Turn the handle right side out and top stitch ⅜″ from each side.

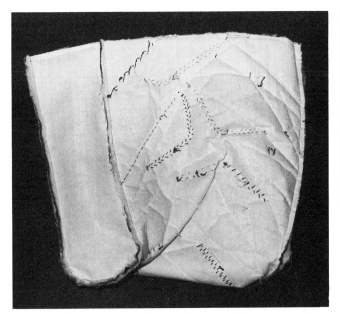

Sew the body of the bag around the sides, following the basting lines on the sides.

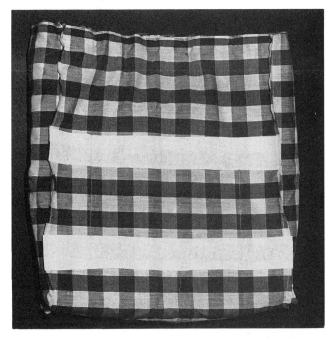

Construct the lining pocket according to the directions for the purse on page 44. Construct the lining in the same manner as the bag, leaving an opening in one side. Pull the lining over the bag, right sides together, and stitch around the top.

Turn the bag right side out. Center the handles on the outside at each side of the bag, 4″ apart, and stitch across several times to fasten them securely.

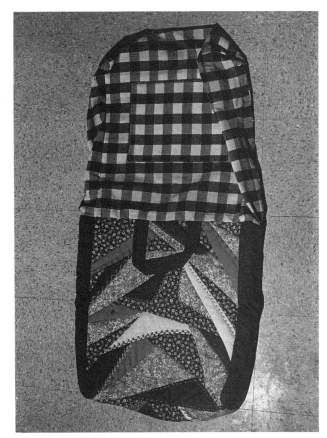

Pull the bag right side out through the opening in the lining. Close the lining and tack it to the bottom of the bag to anchor it in place.

Project

11

Purse

Cutting Directions:

Cut Front (A) and Back & Flap (B) of batting, lining fabric, and nonbias Pellon.

	Small Purse	Large Purse
Boxing for lining:	$2'' \times 26''$	$2'' \times 32''$
Outside handle-boxing		
(see Note 3, below):	$2'' \times 52''$	$2'' \times 66''$
Cut one each of batting, Pellon, and handle fabric. The handle can be pieced.		
Inside handle:	$2'' \times 28''$	$2'' \times 36''$
Cut one of handle fabric.		
Pocket:	$5\frac{1}{2}'' \times 6\frac{1}{2}''$	$6\frac{1}{2}'' \times 7\frac{1}{2}''$
Cut two of lining, one of Pellon.		
Pocket reinforcement:	$1\frac{1}{2}'' \times 10''$	$1\frac{1}{2}'' \times 12''$
Button loop:	$1'' \times 6''$	$1'' \times 6''$

Supplies Needed:

Pellon: heavyweight, nonbias type, ⅔ yard
Lining fabric: ⅓ yard for small purse, ½ yard for large
  purse
Large button

Notes:

1. Do not trim batting from the seam allowance.
2. Heavyweight Pellon makes a very firm purse and is what most people making this purse prefer. For a softer, though still firm, purse use regular-weight Pellon. *Never* use all-bias Pellon.
3. The term "handle-boxing" refers to the fact that the boxing around the bottom of the purse and the outside handle is cut as one piece. It's awkward nomenclature, but it gives a secure handle!
4. The handle on the small purse was designed for a young girl. If you wish to lengthen the handle to a size more appropriate for adults, add the same amount of length to the figures for both the outside handle-boxing and the inside handle. To shorten the handle for a nonshoulder strap, shorten the two figures equally.
5. Crazy quilt the purse front (A) first. This makes it possible to plan the fabric placement on the flap so that it will complement the front where it overlaps.
6. Spray with Scotchgard when finished and after each washing.

This pattern makes two sizes of purses, fully lined with an interior pocket. If you're tired of saggy fabric purses, this one is for you! It keeps its shape even after washing. Don't be intimidated by the length of the directions; the amount of detail is to ensure your success.

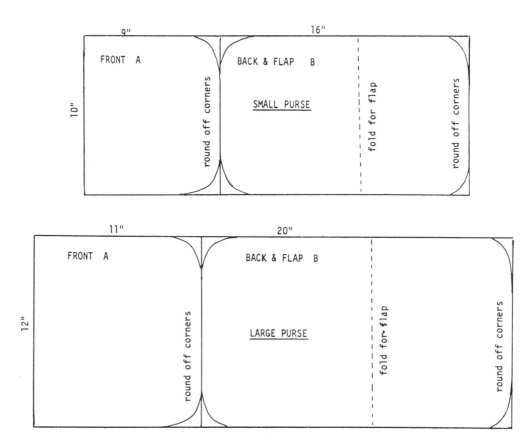

Pattern diagrams for small and large purses.

Construct a blank with Pellon and batting, according to the general instructions. Crazy quilt it, then embroider as desired.

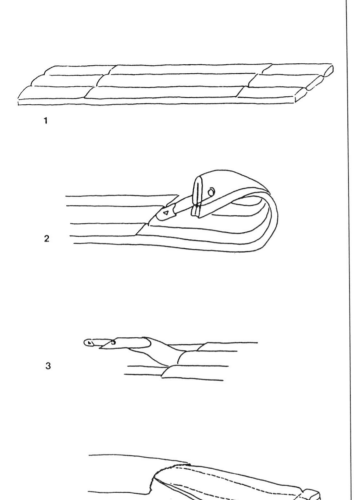

Lay the front on the back flap and mark where the top of the front falls. This is the fold line for the flap. The handle-boxing will be fastened to the purse back as far as this mark.

Make the handle. Center the inside handle on the outside handle-boxing, with the right sides together. Place it on the batting with the Pellon on the bottom. Stitch together the full length on both sides (1), sewing in the same direction to avoid twisting. Attach a large safety pin to one end of the handle and pull it through between the inside handle and the handle-boxing to turn (2 and 3). Press it and join it into a loop (4).

Center the handle-boxing seam at the bottom of the purse front with the right sides together. Stitch, sewing with the handle on top and following the stitching lines on the handle.

Leave the top ¼″ unstitched for ease in applying the lining. You will have to rip the inside handle back approximately 1″ to fit. Leave this flap loose.

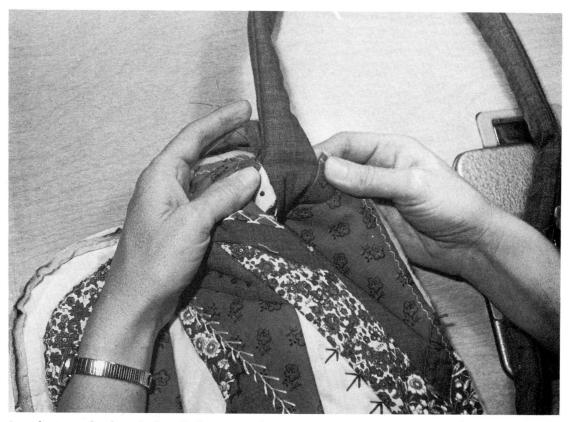

Sew the purse back to the handle-boxing in the same manner, ending ¼″ below the flap's fold line. The seams on the back and front should end exactly across the handle from each other, or else the flap will hang crooked.

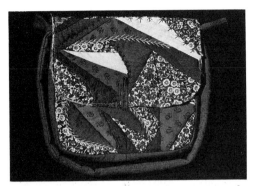

Make a loop for the button and baste it to the flap's center on the right side. Pull the handle down to the bottom of the purse.

Make the lining pocket. Lay the pocket pieces, right sides together, under the Pellon interfacing. Stitch on three sides and turn, leaving the bottom open. Turn under the unstitched side and pin it. Place the pocket on the lining back about 2″ below the flap's fold line. Reinforce on the wrong side of the lining with Pellon strips across the bottom and top of the pocket. Stitch the pocket into position.

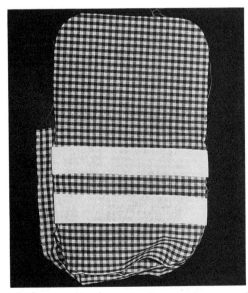

Sew the lining boxing to the lining front and back, including the pocket reinforcement in the seam. Leave the seam open on one side of the boxing across the bottom, and leave ¼″ unstitched at the top of the boxing.

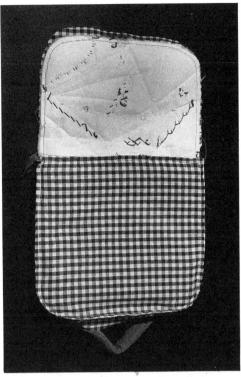

Fit the lining over the purse with the right sides together. Be sure the handle is pulled to the bottom of the purse. Stitch across the front. *Do not* stitch across the boxing. Pull the lining tightly across the flap so that it will not roll to the front when turned. Stitch from the boxing top around the flap to the other side.

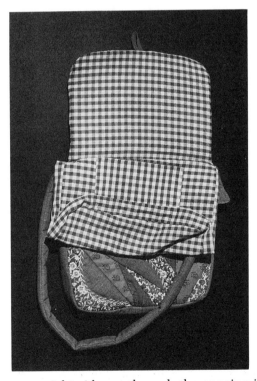

Turn purse right side out through the opening in the lining. Close the opening. Push the lining to the inside of the purse and press the edges.

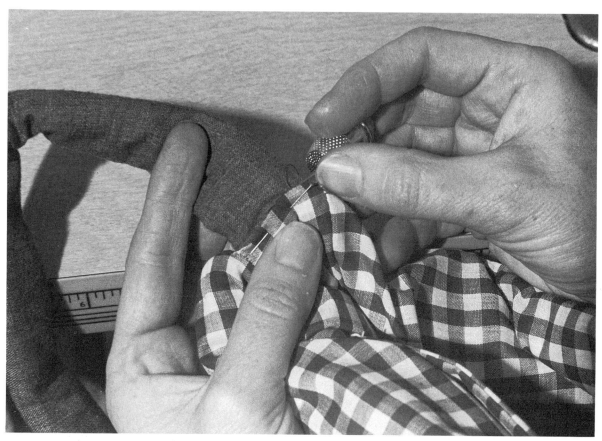

Slip the loose end of the inside handle into the lining boxing and sew it closed. Sew the button in place through the lining.

Project

12

Tablecloth

Cutting Directions:

Crazy quilted sections: Cut four of batting and blank fabric from pattern.

Center square: 4½". Cut one of batting and blank fabric.

Solid-color strips: 1½" × 34½". Cut four of batting and the desired fabric.

Lining: Use the tablecloth for a pattern after the top is completed.

Yardage:

Fabric for blank: 4 yards of 36" muslin.

Lining and solid-color strips: 4 yards of 45" fabric.

Fabric for crazy quilting: This is somewhat difficult to estimate, since it depends on the number of different fabrics used. In this tablecloth, just four fabrics were used. I used approximately 1½ yards each of two prints and ½ yard each of two solid colors. With more fabrics, less of each would be needed.

Notes:

1. Use a lightweight batting.
2. Trim batting from the seam allowance of the blank before crazy quilting.
3. Stitch a line of machine basting from points **A** to **B** on the pattern diagram for crazy quilted sections after the blank is constructed, to hold batting in place on these large pieces.
4. Solid-color strips can be cut from the selvage edge of the lining yardage. Just be sure that you will have a piece 72" square when lining is cut in two-yard lengths and pieced.

The construction of this 72" circular tablecloth is simple, but the size of the pieces makes the crazy quilting more difficult, so practice on smaller items before you tackle this one.

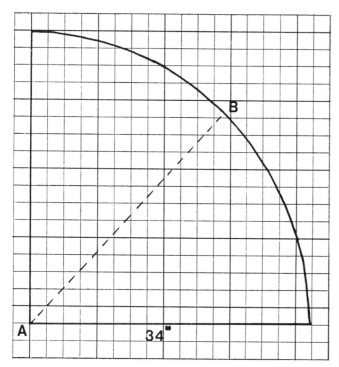

The pattern diagram for the crazy quilted sections of tablecloth. (One square equals two inches.)

Construct the blanks of four quarter-circle sections and the center square, and crazy quilt according to the general instructions. Embroider as desired.

Machine baste the batting to the solid-color strips, using a ¼″ seam allowance. Trim the batting from the seam allowance.

Sew a solid-color strip between two sections of crazy quilting, following the basting stitching on the strips. Sew the small square between the ends of the remaining solid-color strips, making a long center strip. After matching the corners of the solid-color strips and the center square, sew the two halves to either side of the long center strip. Press the seams lightly.

Cut the lining fabric into two-yard lengths and piece it. Use the tablecloth top to cut the lining. Stitch around the edges, leaving a section open for turning. Turn and close the opening by hand. Press the edges lightly. Tack the lining to the top about every 8″, taking care not to let stitches show through the crazy quilting.

Spectacular effects can be achieved with contemporary crazy quilting in clothing. Look at styles with an eye to areas that would be enhanced by quilting. With the following guidelines in mind, you can individualize commercial patterns to be one-of-a-kind originals.

It works best to crazy quilt areas without gathers or darts, and where the added bulk of a quilted section will not accent your own. Small darts can be taken in the blank fabric before the batting is added, but care must be taken when quilting to keep the shape of the blank.

Use a lightweight fabric for the blank and lightweight batting when making clothing. When constructing the blank, use the seam allowance given for the pattern and trim away the batting in the seam allowance so that, when the garment is constructed, the seams will lie flat.

When the pattern pieces to be quilted are close fitting, such as in this shirt, cut the blank ¼" larger on all edges to allow for reduction caused by the quilting. When you have finished crazy quilting, check the completed piece against the pattern and trim it to fit, if necessary. Courtesy, Vogue and Butterick Patterns.

The pattern is shown with top-stitched bandings at the bottom of the sleeve and hem. When using crazy quilting, banding will hang better if it is seamed into the garment with a hem of plain fabric below. Courtesy, Vogue and Butterick Patterns.

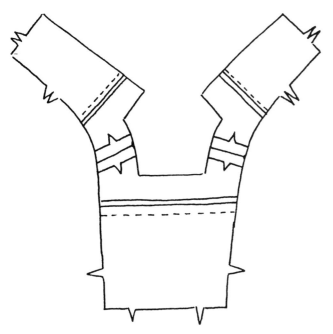

When you have selected the pattern sections to be crazy quilted, join any seams in the blank fabric before adding the batting to the blank. This reduces bulk and gives piecing uninterrupted by seams. In the caftan shown, the crazy quilted section involved four pattern pieces, as shown.

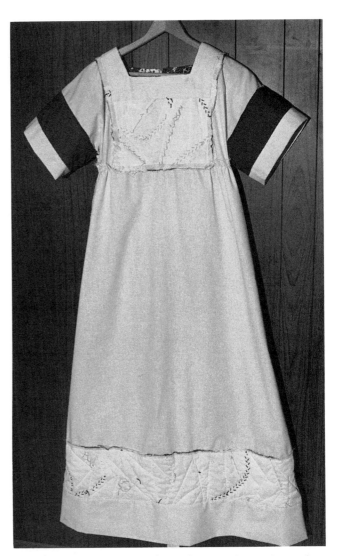

The wrong side of the caftan, showing its construction. The hem below the crazy quilted bands should be cut double the width desired and then folded up to the quilted section. This gives body, which keeps the hem from being distorted by the weight of the quilting.

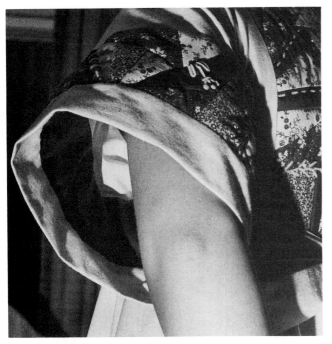

Areas where the wrong side of the quilting will show, such as this sleeve, must be lined with a fabric dark enough to cover any stitchery showing on the wrong side of the blank.

Project

14

Quilt

Yardage:

Gold: Strips for top, back, and bias edging, 10½ yards of 45″ fabric

Brown: Backing for crazy quilted sections, 4⅓ yards of 45″ fabric

Muslin: Fabric for blanks, 5¼ yards of 36″ fabric
Batting: Two, one of which should be 90″ × 108″
Fabric for crazy quilting: 7 yards of fabric

This crazy quilt is truly a quilt. Except for the embroidery, nine seams on the back, and one side of the binding, it is constructed on a sewing machine.

The reverse of the crazy quilt. The fabric that backs the crazy quilted sections must be dark enough to cover the embroidery showing on the back.

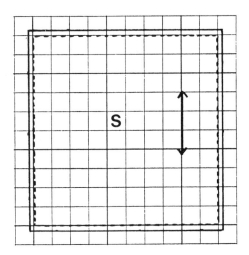

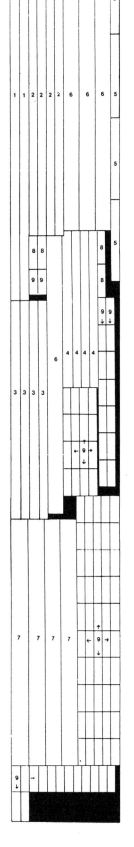

Strip 1:	3½″ × 135″	(cut 2)
Strip 2:	3½″ × 110″	(cut 4)
Strip 3:	3½″ × 85″	(cut 4)
Strip 4:	3½″ × 55″	(cut 4)
Strip 5:	3½″ × 32″	(cut 4)
Strip 6:	6½″ × 106″	(cut 4)
Strip 7:	6½″ × 96″	(cut 4)
Strip 8:	3½″ × 13″	(cut 4)
Strip 9:	3½″ × 10½″	(cut 96)

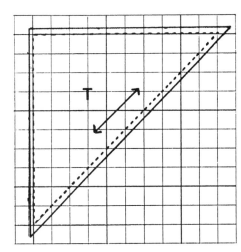

Pattern diagrams for crazy quilted sections. Cut 40 squares and 20 triangles of blank fabric, batting, and backing. (One square equals one inch.)

Cutting chart for the gold strips. The chart covers 9½ yards of fabric. The remaining yard will be used for bias edging. All strips except #9 are cut slightly longer than necessary.

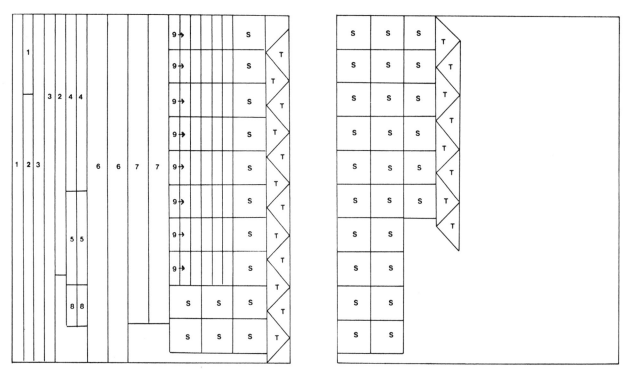

Cutting charts for the batting. Note that strip #1 is pieced. Whip the edges together, taking care to keep them flat and smooth. The charts are worked out for 90″ × 108″ batts, but the second one can be cut from a smaller batt if desired.

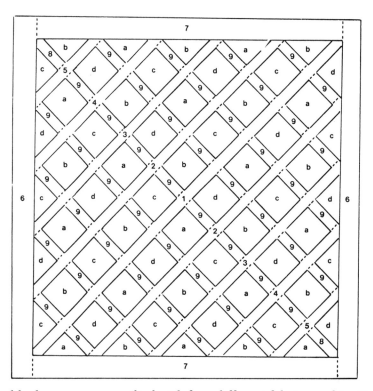

Quilt assembly chart. The blocks were crazy quilted with four different fabric combinations, with ten squares and five triangles of each, designated on the chart as a, b, c, d. If all the blanks are quilted with the same combination of fabrics, disregard these letters on the chart.

   The quilt graphs out at 106″ square, but the actual quilt is 102″. It was made with very puffy batting, which accounts for the difference. If you wish to make the quilt larger or smaller, adjust the size of the crazy quilted sections and the strips to achieve the desired size.

Construct the blank according to the general instructions. Trim the batting from the seam allowances and then crazy quilt, embroidering as desired.

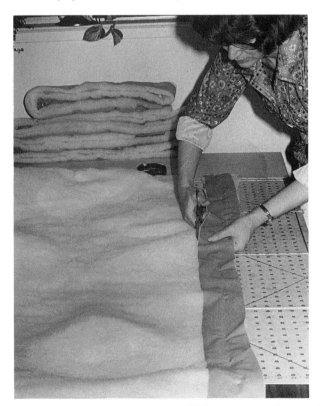

Mark carefully and set aside half the strips, to be used on the back of the quilt. Use the other half to cut batting, using the batting cutting chart as a guide and pinning on each strip as a pattern.

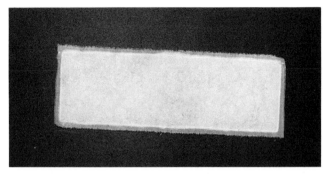

Machine baste the batting to the strips. Trim the batting from the seam allowance on all strips *except* border strips #6 and #7. On these, trim the batting from seam allowance on one side only. The untrimmed sides will be the outside edges of the quilt.

Starting in the upper left-hand corner of the assembly chart, pin the backing to the back of the crazy quilted block. With the right sides together, pin the #8 strip with batting on top of the crazy quilted section and the #8 strip without batting to the backing. (Note on the assembly chart that the #8 strips extend beyond the corners of the quilt blocks.) Stitch, following the machine-basting lines on the strip.

Open out the strips and pin the edges together. With the right sides together, pin the crazy quilted block to the top strip and the backing fabric over the bottom strip. Stitch.

Open out the crazy quilted block and backing, and pin the edges together. This completes the upper left-hand corner row.

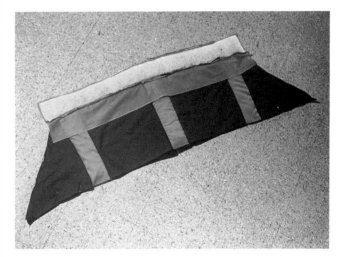

Open out only the top strip. Pin the backing strip out of the way.

Continue constructing diagonal rows in this manner, using #9 strips between blocks except for the lower right-hand corner, which will use a #8 strip.

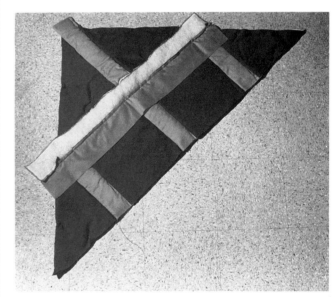

Lining up the short strips, join the top strip to the next completed row, following the machine-basting stitching on the strip.

To join long strips (#1 through #5) to completed rows, sew strips to the longer of the two rows to be joined, on the shortest side of that row.

Close the backing strip by hand. Use the machine stitching as a guide, just covering the stitching with the edge of the backing strip. Continue joining long strips in this manner until the quilt is completed. (Note on the assembly chart that the #1 strip extends beyond the corners of the quilt blocks.)

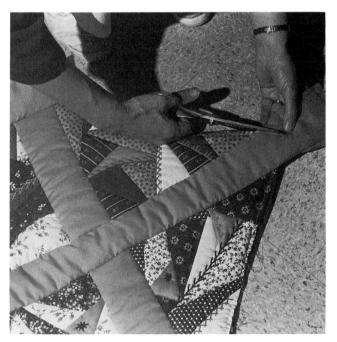

Mark the corners of the quilt on strips #1 and #8, and cut. Trim away the other strips that extend beyond the edge of the quilt.

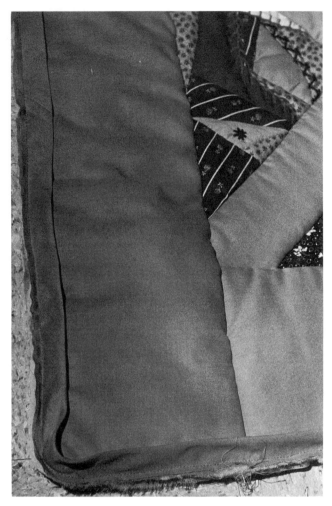

Attach the borders of the quilt, #6 and #7, in the same manner as the strips were added, making sure that the side where the batting was not trimmed from the seam allowance is at the outside edge of the quilt.

Cut a 2″-wide bias from the remaining gold fabric. Fold in half lengthwise and press down the center, taking care not to stretch it. Join it to the top of the quilt, with the raw edges of the bias lined up with the raw edges of the quilt. Round the corners slightly.

Roll the bias over the edge to the wrong side of the quilt, just covering the machine stitching, and close by hand. The bias edges on the front and back of the quilt should be equal. This application gives a strong, even edge to the quilt.

Index

Numbers in italics indicate illustrations